London's First Motor Buses

An album compiled by Mick Webber
with articles from Commercial Motor, The Daily Chronicle, Old Motor and the London Historical Research Group of The Omnibus Society

Capital Transport

First published 2022

ISBN 978 1 85414 472 0

Published by
Capital Transport Publishing Ltd
www.capitaltransport.com

Printed by Parksons Graphics

Front cover: The London Central Motor Omnibus Co was the of the more successful pioneering London motorbus operators and survived until being absorbed into the LGOC in 1913. This Leyland X2, dating from 1908, was fitted with a second-hand 1906 Tilling body, removed from a Milnes-Daimler when Tilling converted several buses to mail vans after winning a contract to run the mails. It was restored from a terribly derelict state by Mike Sutcliffe in 1996 after which he was awarded an MBE for 'Services to Motor Heritage'.

Marble Arch in the 1920s on a fine sunny day. The arch was designed by John Nash in 1827, and was erected near Buckingham Palace as a grand entrance, but when the Palace was enlarged in 1847, the Arch was dismantled and moved to its present site. The bus is B 5053, which is working the long established route 16 between Victoria and Cricklewood, where it will turn and stand on the forecourt of The Crown public house. (Mick Webber Collection)

Thomas Tilling route 13 worked from Bromley to Oxford Circus (shown as Oxford Street on the destination blind) for nine months in 1910. Their fleet number 78 was a 1908 Hallford, and and the location is probably just south of Tweedy Road, with the wall of Bromley College leading away on the left. It was the only bus of this make in the fleet. The route was later renumbered 64, and continued until 1913. The rare sight of a car outside the stationers shop on the left is notable. (Richard Stevenson Collection)

Opposite: Motor Bus routes at May 1913 (London Transport Museum)

CONTENTS

Introduction 7
The Beginnings of Motor Buses 8
A Battle over Registration Numbers 14
The Training of a Motor Bus Driver 18
Developments and New Ideas 26
Electric Buses 32
The B Type 36
The Next Developments 54
The New Independents - 1922 64
Second to None 74

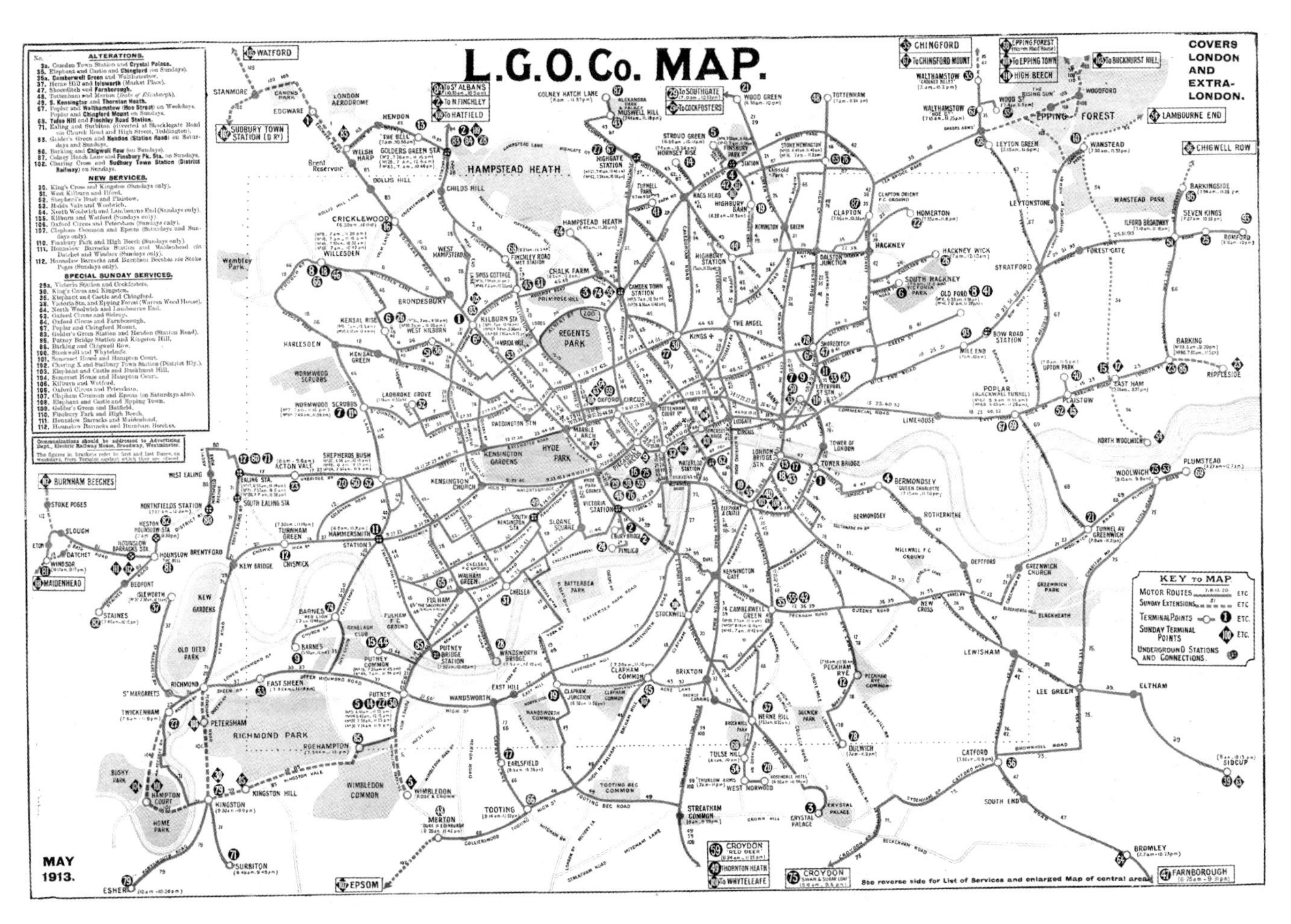

There was no connection between the horse tramways of the North Metropolitan Tramways Company along Upper Clapton Road and Lower Clapton Road and those of the Lea Bridge, Leyton & Walthamstow Tramways Company along Lea Bridge Road. However, the latter company operated a significant network of horse bus routes to connect with its tram routes, and it likely to be one their buses that is seen in the background of this view. This junction has been replaced by a large roundabout, and is unrecognisable today.

Introduction

Queen Victoria, in the 64th year of her reign, just managed to survive into the 20th Century and her death in January 1901 can truly be described as the end of an era.

The modern world was dawning. The early 1900s were a time of great optimism about the future, brought suddenly and tragically to an end in July 1914 with the start of the Great War. In 1903, the first London County Council electric tram was introduced, leading to a large system of electric trams in Greater London over the next 11 years. The year 1903 also saw the first aeroplane flight.

The first reliable petrol-driven motor bus was introduced in London in 1904, with all horse drawn buses in the capital withdrawn by 1911. The years 1906 and 1907 saw a big growth in the tube railways, with three new lines, Bakerloo, Piccadilly and part of today's Northern Line, introduced. Also in 1907, the first synthetic plastic, polyoxybenzylmethylenglycolanhydride, was invented by a Belgian chemist. It was 'the material of a thousand uses' according to its publicity and was marketed as Bakelite.

In the following year, Henry Ford introduced in America (without any of the new plastic) the first affordable mass-produced car. The car began to be made in England in 1913. 'Affordable' is a relative term of course and it generally applied in this case to upper middle classes in the UK. In 1913 – the last year before war almost completely halted production - 16,000 cars were produced in the UK, mainly by Ford and Austin, bringing the total cars in use here up to about 100,000. The great majority of citizens used a bike or public transport to get anywhere beyond walking distance.

Home entertainment was mostly self-generated at the start of the century, a common piece of furniture, even in poorer homes where much was second hand, being the upright piano. Gramophones began to be popular among middle classes from 1901 with the first 78rpm shellac records enabling the finest professional singers, among others, to be heard in the living room of any home with one of these new wind-up machines. Radio was over 20 years in the future and television for the masses around 50 years away. For those who could afford it there were theatres to go to, but easier on the pocket were skating rinks, dance and music halls and the new cinemas showing silent films to the musical accompaniment of a pianist.

Film cameras began to be used in some numbers at the beginning of the century. Kodak's famous Brownie was introduced in the UK in 1900 and led to a big growth in amateur photography, with the first 35mm camera being introduced in 1913 following its patenting in 1908. All the photographs in this album were taken by professionals however, using tripod cameras with large glass-plate negatives. Thanks are due to the help provided by Andrew Robertson and Mike Sutcliffe in the compilation of this album.

Left: The Associated Omnibus Company began operating horse buses in November 1900. They worked from premises in Camden Town, and began working motor buses in May 1905. Three of their horse buses are pictured here at Muswell Hill Broadway on route 79, which worked to Victoria, as did the LGOC motorbus behind them on route 4, which commenced on 1st April 1912. (Richard Stevenson Collection)

The Beginnings of Motor Buses

Andrew Robertson

At the end of the nineteenth century road traffic in London was almost entirely horse-powered. The Locomotives on Highways Act 1896, which famously abolished the requirement for a motor vehicle to be preceded by a man on foot carrying a red flag, began the development of motor cars on U.K. roads as a practical form of transport, but the technology of the time struggled to produce larger vehicles suitable for commercial operation. In addition the conservative approach of the Public Carriage Office of the Metropolitan Police, the licensing authority was a hindrance to the development of motor buses.

After various experimental omnibuses powered by batteries or by steam had been licensed but never operated in service, the first motor bus service in London started on 9th October 1899, when the Motor Traction Company Ltd started operating two petrol-engined 24-seat double-deck buses between Kennington Gate and Victoria Station via Westminster Bridge. Operation was from a garage at 26/27 Walnut Tree Walk Kennington, but only lasted until December 1900.

In December 1900 the established horse bus operator London Road-Car Company Ltd introduced one experimental motor bus on a similarly short-lived service between Hammersmith, Shepherd's Bush and Oxford Circus; it was withdrawn in March 1901.

After various small operators began short-lived services using wagonettes (small single-deckers typically seating eight or ten passengers) which ran between 1901 and 1903, London Road-Car began another trial on 17th March 1902 using a Thornycroft steam chassis with a 36-seat double-deck body; this operated the same Hammersmith to Oxford Circus route as previously but only ran until 19th April.

The next motor bus operator was C.C. Dennis, who began a route between Eltham and Lee Green on 3rd October 1902. This used a petrol engined double-deck bus with a 27-seat double-deck body which was designed by the noted motor car pioneer Harry John Lawson. It was noteworthy as the first large bus to be fitted with (solid) rubber tyres (earlier buses used steel tyres), and it ran until early 1904.

With the concept of a reliable double-deck bus remaining problematic, the next stage of development in London was that of small single-deckers. The London Motor Omnibus Syndicate Ltd introduced a service between Cricklewood and Oxford Circus on 26th November 1902 using four 12-seat petrol-engined Stirling buses. This service last ran on 27th August 1903, but the company was reconstituted as the London Power Omnibus Company which started a service between Kilburn and Marble Arch on 15th February 1904 with a fleet of seven single-deck buses, including two from the the London Motor Omnibus's original fleet.

London Road-Car began another motor bus trial on 8th October 1904, this time using two Chelmsford (a manufacturer later better known as Clarkson) paraffin-fuelled steam single-deckers with 14-seat bodies, running on a Hammersmith to Oxford Circus route similar to its earlier motorbus experiments. London's largest bus operator, the London General Omnibus Company Ltd, began its first motorbus service two days later, using a similar Chelmsford steamer running between Hammersmith and Piccadilly Circus via Kensington. The LGOC had experimented the previous year with an American Fischer petrol-electric bus, but the petrol consumption and tyre wear were so great it never entered service.

Meanwhile leading tramcar manufacturer George F. Milnes & Company had begun to import German Daimler bus chassis which they assembled and marketed to the British market as Milnes-Daimler. After initial success with a chassis for single-deckers, a double-deck version appeared at the Crystal Palace Motor Car Show in February 1904. One of these was ordered by established horse bus operator Thomas Tilling and fitted with a 34-seat double-deck body built by Birch Bros, who were significant horse bus operators themselves as well as bodybuilders. The body established the basic style of London motorbus bodies until the First World War.

Tilling introduced this bus on the existing Peckham to Oxford Circus route on 30th September, replacing two horse buses. At the time typical horse buses seated 26. A photograph of a bus with similar bodywork will be found on page 24 of this book. Operation was successful, and Birch Bros bought and bodied two similar chassis of their own, which entered service on the existing horse bus route between Baker Street Station and Waterloo Station on 11th October 1904.

At the end of 1904 there were just twenty motorbuses licensed to operate in the Metropolitan Police area, but their technical development had now reached the point where commercial operation to replace horse buses had become a practical proposition and their number was soon to increase rapidly.

The London Motor Omnibus Syndicate Ltd introduced a service between Oxford Circus and Cricklewood on 26th November 1902 using four 12-seat Stirling single-deckers, as seen here, in the days before registration plates were required. The service last ran on 27th August 1903, but the business was reorganised and subsequently resumed operation as the London Power Omnibus Company. (Roger Warwick Collection)

The first large bus in London to be fitted with rubber (rather than steel) tyres was this petrol-engined Canstatt-Daimler, with a body designed by early motor pioneer Harry John Lawson. It was operated by Charles Claude Dennis on a route between Lee Green and Eltham, which ran between October 1902 and early 1904.

The first Leyland petrol driven bus was this Y type, with Crossley 4-cyl 22/30hp engine, a double-decker seating 34 (plus 2 by the driver) with body by Scammell & Nephew. It was painted in the blue, yellow and red livery of The New London & Suburban Omnibus Co Ltd, a London operator of horse buses, and was lettered 'A' in their fleet (using letters rather than fleet numbers), registered in Surrey, P 1944. It was delivered just in time to be exhibited at the 10th Cordingley's Show, held annually at the Royal Agricultural Hall, Islington, 18th – 25th March 1905, then ran on a route from Surbiton to Kew Bridge. The company went bankrupt and re-formed as London Central MOC, then re-formed twice more before being sold with about 100 Leylands to the LGOC in 1913. (Mike Sutcliffe Collection)

The LGOC's very first motor bus was this Fischer petrol-electric, imported from the USA, which was delivered in April 1903 and bodied by the LGOC. Petrol consumption and tyre wear were so great that no attempt was made to place it in service, and in October 1903 the LGOC sought to return the chassis to the manufacturer and reclaim its £450 purchase price.

Number 6 in the London Road-Car Company's motor bus fleet was this Straker-Bussing, new in March 1905. (Mike Sutcliffe Collection)

London Road-Car Company also experimented with this Chelmsford steam bus which entered service in September 1905. Shortly afterwards London Road-Car Company began using the fleetname Union Jack. The Chelmsford company was later renamed Clarkson, by which name it became better known. This is LC 2320. (Mike Sutcliffe Collection)

A Battle Over Registration Numbers

Bernard Brown

On 28th April 1904 correspondence was received at the Public Carriage Office from Middlesex County Council as to the fact that motor buses were running along High Road Kilburn without the new registration plates as required under the Act of 1903 and therefore did not carry an illuminated lamp to the rear. A reply was sent back from the PCO on 30 April 1904 by none other than Chief Inspector Bassom who was later to be responsible for the suffix lettering scheme on London's bus services (1924-1934). Surprisingly, Bassom took the view that the vehicles in question need not comply with the new Act as they were already identifiable by the Metropolitan Stage Carriage plate number painted on the vehicles. He thought the imposition of a motor car registration plate would lead to confusion, and in any case the motor buses were running on a regular and well-lit route on the Edgware Road. In addition he pointed out that each driver was identified by a motor driver's or mechanical power tin badge.

All this attention was caused by the motor buses of the London Motor Power Company, who had opened a route in February 1904 between Kilburn and Marble Arch. Shortly after, the London County Council (who issued the letter A registrations) also complained to Scotland Yard about these unregistered motor buses along High Road Kilburn, just as Middlesex County Council had done and who, incidentally, issued the letter H for mechanically propelled vehicles.

At the heart of the matter was a dispute over loss of revenue in licensing the motor buses, and came about due to the fact that High Road Kilburn was in reality a sort of 'no man's land' due to one side being in Willesden Parish (part of Middlesex) while the other was firmly in "the smoke" as part of the Metropolitan Borough of Hampstead and in LCC territory. In order to clarify the matter a report was sent to the Under Secretary of State at the Home Office so that the new legislation could be looked into. Bassom took it upon himself to pass the following edict and stated to the Councils concerned that 'I consider that the present means of identification (i.e. MSC plate) is adequate'.

Meanwhile both the LCC and MCC appealed to the Commissioner of Police, Sir Edward Henry, about Bassom's interpretation of the Act, pointing out that while the Police Plate is often exchanged with other vehicles, the new motor car plate was a permanent means of tracing ownership through the respective council (and of course another form of revenue by charging a search fee).

Bassom stuck by his guns but on 20th January 1905 poor Bassom received a flea in his ear when the report returned from the Home Office, which in strong terms said 'It is not for the Police to question the validity of any Act and they will hereafter enforce any infringements of the said Motor Car Act 1903'.

The following month suitable apologies were sent to both County Councils by Mr Bassom. However, this little known incident does not appear to have affected his career as he remained in the Public Carriage Office, later holding the rank of Chief Constable. He died in January 1926 at the age of only 59 years but he was a Londoner only by adoption, coming originally from Whittlesford near Cambridge.

The London Power Omnibus Company was formed in 1904, and its vehicles carried the fleet name Pioneer. This is LC 2625, a Scott-Stirling vehicle, turning into Regent Street on its route from Charing Cross to Cricklewood. The company was based at Kilburn, but had gone bankrupt by 1907. (Mike Sutcliffe Collection)

The Victoria Omnibus Co. Ltd was formed by members of the Victoria Station Association of horse bus proprietors. It began operation on 27th July 1905 between Kilburn and Marble Arch, on what was later to become route 16, using Swiss-built Orion buses. The route was extended from Marble Arch to Victoria on 6th September 1905, and from Kilburn to Cricklewood on 14th March 1906, but the Victoria company ceased operations after 17th July 1907. One of the Orions, LC 2365, is seen here at Victoria Station. (Roger Warwick Collection)

London Standard Motor Omnibus Company owned seven vehicles in their brief existence between 1906 and 1907. LC 6677 was a Lacoste Battmann from 1905, and displays details of their route from Finsbury Park to Hammersmith.

A 9008 is a Straker-Squire that entered service with the LGOC in 1905. It is operating on what became route 16, which still follows the same route today. Note the horse bus style livery with the termini of the route painted on the side panel. Lord Palmerston is the name of the terminal point, a pub at Kilburn. (Roger Warwick Collection)

The Training of a Motor Bus Driver

from *The Daily Chronicle*

Every motor bus driver employed by the London General Omnibus Company Limited, before he is allowed to ply the streets, receives about three months schooling. This schooling does not simply entail lessons in driving, but involves a most thorough grounding in the anatomy of the engines. And so it comes about that at the end of his studies the motor bus has no little nerve that is not known and understood by the driver. Thus the driver is not only the motor's guide, philosopher and friend, but physician and surgeon all in one. And the result is a minimum of noise and smell and freedom from serious accident.

The system of training was introduced by Mr J.H. Fooks-Bale, the manager of the motor department at the Dollis Hill garage, Cricklewood. There are two schools, the theory being taught at the Torrens Street depot Islington, and in the Cricklewood garage lessons are given in driving. A winding sawdust-strewn gangway leads one to the Torrens Street school, and as you go up at every corner you find a stableman grooming down a patient my-time-has-come-looking sort of horse. And right at the top of the building you enter a large stable. But though there are many things – mangers, hay racks, cornbins, kicking "bales", broken horse-shoes, saddle pegs, no horse is there. Ousted! Instead thereof, in the middle of the room, rests a Wolseley motor. And insult is added to injury, in that the usurper is supported by a couple of corn bins ballasted with water-filled mangers and, insult of all, the interloper using a manger as a cooling tank! No wonder the horses on the gangway are wrapped in Byronic gloom!

Fronting the engine is a raised platform and a large blackboard, on which fearsome-looking diagrams are drawn by an expert instructor, and ranged round the platform are the pupils, men who are still driving horse buses, who listen intently and intelligently to lessons in applied science. The engine under dissection is a 14 horse-power two-cylinder Wolseley, fitted with high-tension battery ignition and also high-tension magneto. It is arranged with fly-wheel suitable for making brake tests of any horse power developed under varying circumstances. All this is explained most lucidly by the instructor, Mr F. Bryan, AICE. He purposely throws the engine out of gear, and calls upon a pupil to diagnose and treat accordingly. Something is touched and the dead comes to life. The water in the ballast tanks ripples, the stable shakes, the engine coughs and spits and bubbles rise in the cooling tank. And the how, when and where and why of it all is carefully explained. Too much oil is fed into the machine; and immediately the air stinks, and the place is filled with smoke. In turn, the wretched engine is made to suffer every ill – and there be many – to which a motor is a natural heir.

Since the Handcross disaster particular attention has been paid to the action of the brakes. Half the troubles with brakes arise from ignorance and the other half from carelessness. A well-trained driver ought to have as much feeling in his toes as ordinary folk have in their fingers. An expert driver knows the value of free-wheeling; and always has as much brake power as possible in reserve. Brakes are frequently rendered inoperative through leakage of oil, but nothing more than a little petrol is needed to make the surface perfectly clean. At every lesson, Mr Bryan insists upon the vital importance of a thorough overhauling by the driver of all brakes before the car is taken out of the garage.

At the present time there are some fifty men undergoing instruction at Torrens Street, the lessons being held twice daily and of two hours' duration. One shift attends in the morning and another in the evening. For the remainder of the day the men go back to their horse-buses. After spending from one to two months in the technical school, the men are sent to the Dollis Hill garage and are there made familiar in every possible way with the motor buses they are destined to drive. They are divided into classes of six, each class having its own instructor, and the lessons are carried out in the same practical fashion as at Torrens Street. Every day the instructor takes his class for trial drives, and each man in turn handles the driving wheel. As a man becomes more proficient, test accidents are arranged, baulks of wood, stones, barrels and so forth being suddenly thrown across his track. And in due course Scotland Yard passes him as competent to drive.

Since last March, 130 men have passed through the schools, at the cost to the company of nearly £200 per week, and there are about 40 trained drivers waiting for new buses when they can be supplied.

Accompanying the article was an official notice, the text of which runs:

LONDON GENERAL OMNIBUS COMPANY LIMITED

NOTICE TO MOTOR OMNIBUS DRIVERS

It is desirable that all drivers should know as much as possible about the engine, *et cetera*, of which they are in charge. With this object in view arrangements have been made for a Training School at Dollis Hill garage, and Drivers will be expected to attend the morning or evening classes of the school at least one hour per day. Those engaged on afternoon shift can receive the instruction from 10 to 12 am, and those engaged on the morning shift from 6 to 8 pm. Men engaged at other Garages belonging to the Company must attend at Dollis Hill for the present at the times stated above.

J.H. FOOKS-BALE, manager of the Motor Department, Dollis Hill garage.

Joseph Clough, known as Joe to his friends and family, was London's first black bus driver. Born in Jamaica in 1887, in 1910 he joined the London General Omnibus Company and trained at Shepherd's Bush garage. After completing his training, Joe became a spare driver, driving different routes when needed. He then became a regular driver on bus route 11, operating between Liverpool Street and Wormwood Scrubs. Although generally accepted by his colleagues, Joe was wrongfully suspended for speeding by a racist company official. His excellent driving record and good character led to his rapid reinstatement. It was not the last time he encountered racism, whether casual or overt. Joe worked as an LGOC driver until just before the First World War, when he moved out of London. (London Transport Museum)

LN 2272 was the last of six Leyland X types delivered in late 1907 to the London Central Motor Omnibus Company. The company was formed in 1906, and lasted until 1912. The route worked here from Chalk Farm to Camberwell Green, later became the 68 and worked well into London Transport years. This view is at the Aldwych, facing the Strand. The building on the left, is the Gaiety theatre, which opened in 1903, and was demolished in 1958. (Mike Sutcliffe Collection)

Arrow was the fleetname of the London & District Motor Bus Company, which was an associate company of Vanguard and was absorbed by Vanguard in 1907. LC 2241 is a Lacoste-Battman dating from July 1906, and it is seen operating Arrow's route between Putney Station and Shoreditch (Bell), which evolved into today's route 9. The prominent white arrow above the driver's canopy will be noted. (Mike Sutcliffe Collection)

The Premier Omnibus Company Ltd (not to be confused with the later Premier company which began operating in 1923) was one of the last of the first generation of independent operators in London. It commenced operation on 23rd October 1913 operating an unnumbered route between Liverpool Street and Victoria identical to LGOC route 11. It was renamed the London Premier Omnibus Co. Ltd in May 1914, and last operated on 26th November 1916. With the driver's tarpaulin in use, it has presumably been raining, but none of the passengers seem to be using theirs. This is a DeDion 30hp, LF 9943. (Mike Sutcliffe Collection)

The London & Westminster Motor Omnibus Co. Ltd was a short-lived operator which used the fleetname Ensign. It operated this route between Hammersmith and Piccadilly Circus, starting on 1st July 1906, followed by another between Hammersmith and Finsbury Park in September, but ran into financial difficulties later the same year and was dissolved in 1907. This Ducommun carried a Hora body. (Mike Sutcliffe Collection)

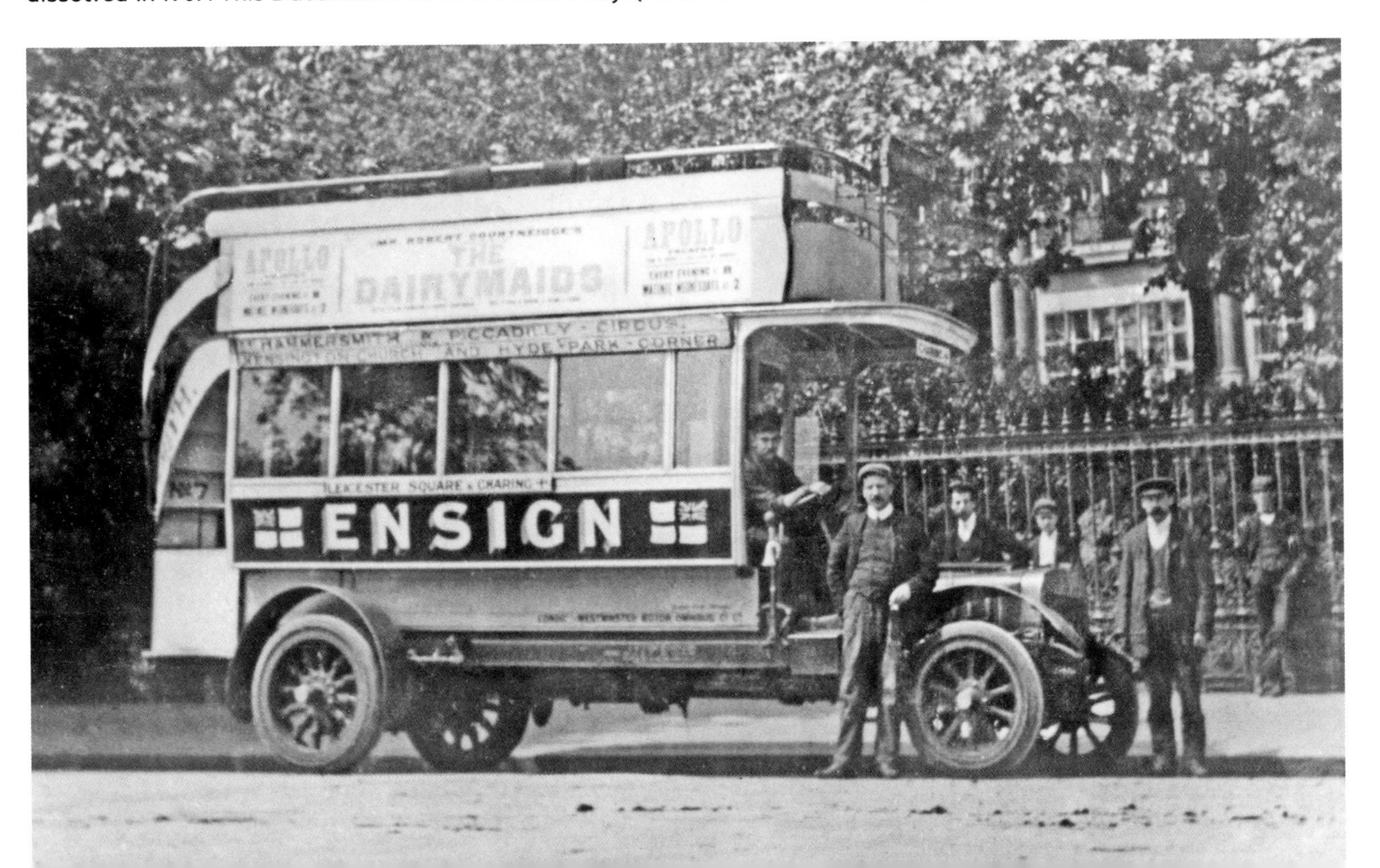

The London Road-Car Company was based in south west London and founded in 1880. It started operating motor buses in 1904, and continued to do so until 1908, when it was amalgamated with the LGOC. The vehicle in this view is a Straker-Squire, and is working the 20 to West Norwood in Norwood Road, Tulse Hill. London Road-Car used letters instead of numbers to designate their routes, and this had been route T, but numbers were allocated when the amalgamation with the LGOC took place. One of the shops on the right is proudly titled as "Cigar stores and toilet saloon". The multiple adverts on the end wall of the terrace to the right was a common sight. (Richard Stevenson Collection)

BE SURE IT'S
VELMA
CHOCOLATE
Rowntree
FLAVOUR
FORCE
makes life sunny
KENNINGTON THEATRE, S.E.
MITCHAM
D'OYLY CARTE
WELSBACH
LIGHT
BORN
1820
CIGAR STORES &
TOILET SALOON.
SHAVING
SALOON
SHAVING
TELEPHONE
CARTER
PATERSON
POULTRY STORES
GINGER BEER

This is the junction of Lee High Road and Burnt Ash Lane at Lee Green. The impressive terrace facing the camera is still happily intact, and the "Old Tigers Head" occupies the right hand end. The "New Tigers Head" is just out of shot on the right, and whilst it survives, it is no longer a pub. Much is going on here. A horse bus is terminating before returning to Penge. The main vehicle here is A 8759, which is number 6 in the Thomas Tilling fleet, and is a Milnes Daimler, new in April 1905. The bus looks very fragile as it leans under the weight of boarding passengers bound for Eltham and Sidcup.

The Great Eastern London Suburban Tramways and Omnibus Company began in May 1900, and in June 1905, it began motor bus operations from its Forest Gate base. In March 1906 the motor bus business was reconstituted as the Great Eastern London Motor Omnibus Company Ltd, whose fleet rose to 81, until it was amalgamated with the LGOC in April 1911 following protracted negotiations. AN 445 was a Dennis 24hp with worm-driven axle, new in March 1906. It was later replaced by a Straker-Squire and almost certainly given the body off the Dennis, with the registration number going with the body as frequently happened in the early days. (London Transport Museum)

Developments and New Ideas

Andrew Robertson

Following the successful debut in service of the Milnes-Daimler double-decker, the practicability of motorbus operation was boosted by the Heavy Motor Car Order 1904, which increased the permitted unladen weight of buses to five tons from 1st March 1905, with a permitted maximum speed of 12 mph.

Thomas Tilling quickly ordered a further twenty-four Milnes Daimlers, while Birch Bros ordered three more. Meanwhile new competitors were inspired to enter into the London motorbus business, of which the first was the London Motor Omnibus Company Ltd, who commenced operation on 27th March 1905 with a fleet of five Milnes-Daimlers. This company pioneered the use of a distinctive name shown prominently on the side of the bus, as what became known as a fleetname, choosing the name Vanguard. Around the same time the London Power Omnibus Company began using the fleetname Pioneer. Shortly afterwards, London Road-Car Company adopted the fleetname Union Jack, while LGOC used the fleetname General.

Another important innovation introduced by Vanguard was the route number, first used on 23rd April 1906; before then, like the horse bus services they were starting to replace, routes were identified only by reference to the termini between which they operated.

The LGOC and the London Road-Car Company also now started full scale motorbus services. Motorbus operation grew during 1905, with more existing horse bus operators, such as Associated Omnibus Company, Balls Brothers and P. Hearn starting motorbus operation, as well as new operators such as London & Provincial (Arrow), Motor Bus Company (Pilot) and New London & Suburban Omnibus Company. However, at the end of 1905 there were still only around 230 motorbuses licensed in London.

Most early motor buses in London used European chassis from such manufacturers as Büssing, de Dion, Durkopp, Germain, Lacoste-Battman, Orion and Scheibler. One of the most popular and successful early chassis was the Straker-Squire, manufactured in the UK using Büssing patents.

Although the petrol engine dominated, it was not yet reliable, and it was by no means clear at this stage that the internal combustion engine would achieve the monopoly of road transport that it later did. The early steam vehicles produced by Thomas Clarkson's Chelmsford company have already been mentioned. Clarkson was convinced that paraffin-fired steam vehicles were a viable alternative to petrol engines, and the National Steam Car Company, which Clarkson originally formed as a means to demonstrate his buses, operated Clarkson steam buses successfully on a small network of routes in London between 1909 and 1919. The Metropolitan Steam Omnibus Company was the other significant operator of steam buses in London, commencing in October 1907 using French Darracq-Serpolet chassis. This used a higher-pressure boiler termed a flash boiler. Operating difficulties with these buses caused Metropolitan Steam to switch to petrol-engined buses in 1912, although the company name continued unchanged.

Another alternative to the conventional bus was the petrol-electric bus, at the time sometimes termed gearless, whereby a petrol engine drove a generator which supplied electric current to motors driving

The Gearless Omnibus Co. Ltd was formed in 1906 to operate buses using a patented transmission system, to be built by Daimler. Only one bus was completed, and it never entered service. The company, in which Daimler held a controlling interest, was then dormant until Daimler were contracted to supply buses to the Tramways (MET) Omnibus Co. Ltd, who ordered 22 buses to be operated by Gearless. By the time they were delivered the Tramways (MET) Omnibus Co. Ltd had entered into an operating agreement with the LGOC's parent company the Underground Group, and the Gearless Daimlers entered service in April 1913 alongside MET Daimlers operating route 13 from Hendon garage. Here the driver of LF 9855 (later to become D 253 in the LGOC fleet) exchanges words with a delivery boy on a tricycle. LGOC B 1735 alongside is on route 11. Gearless used an off-white livery for its buses, which must have stood out in London's traffic.

the rear wheels. The largest operator of petrol-electric buses was Thomas Tilling, who first introduced an experimental design in January 1908. The first production petrol-electrics were the Tilling-Stevens TTA1, which started entering service in June 1911. Thereafter Tillings used only petrol-electrics in London until replacement by conventional petrol-engined buses began in 1930.

The other major alternative to the petrol engine was the battery electric bus, which is dealt with in the next chapter.

By the end of 1906 there were almost 800 motor buses operating in London, and the number had passed the 1,000 mark in March 1908. A significant event shortly afterwards was the amalgamation from 1st July 1908 of LGOC, Vanguard and London Road-Car into an enlarged LGOC which was immediately the dominant operator in London, owning 882 out of a total by now of 1,063 motor buses operating in London. The enlarged company applied the Vanguard numbering system to all its routes from 2nd November 1908, although the route network was still small with 20 being the highest number in use for motorbuses. There were still 62 LGOC horse bus routes at this date, which were given numbers from 31 upwards at the same time. However, the replacement of horse bus routes by motorbus operation was gathering pace, with the number of

Thomas Clarkson's National Steam Car Co. Ltd was originally formed to develop and build his designs for paraffin-fuelled steam motor vehicles, but having experienced difficulty with sales he decided to move into bus operation as a way of demonstrating the practicality of his designs. Bus operation in London started in 2nd November 1909 on a route between Shepherd's Bush and Westminster Bridge Road, but this view shows F 7381 on a private hire working. (Mike Sutcliffe Collection)

The George and Dragon at Farnborough in Kent, was a bus terminus for many years, and the long trunk route 47 to Shoreditch was its main occupant. Thomas Tilling operated the route from the garage at Victory Place, Lewisham, and later Catford. The pub shown in this view, was demolished and rebuilt in 1937, and that in turn, was demolished for housing in 2004. The two identifiable buses in this view are LF 9022 and LC 4144, both Tilling-Stevens TTA1 petrol electrics, and were numbered 211 and 201 in the fleet. Tilling's London bus operations together with 369 buses passed to the LPTB in October 1933. (Roger Warwick Collection)

W P Allen was an early motorbus pioneer, with operations at various times in Farningham (as Dartford & District Motor Services and Farningham & District), Great Yarmouth and in Worcestershire. He operated in London under the name Allen Motor Omnibus Co. Ltd, between January 1914 and November 1916. This was an Edison 40hp battery-electric bus with Dodson-built 'Allen-type' body, new in November 1915 and was used to demonstrate the Beck Patent Collapsible Hood, and it probably never ran in service. (Mike Sutcliffe Collection)

Ten of the Gearless Daimlers were requisitioned by the War Department in World War I, and in partial replacement ten new B-types were assembled by AEC from spare parts in 1916, and were given very high fleet numbers; there was a gap in the numbering sequence from B 5134 to B 6865. In this view B 6875 is operating from Mortlake garage on a short working to Hammersmith on route 9.

motorbuses licensed equalling the number of horsebuses by 31st October 1910, and the last LGOC horse buses ran on 25th October 1911. The last horse buses of all in London, operated by Thomas Tilling, ran on 4th August 1914.

In August 1909 new regulations reduced the maximum permitted weight of buses to 3.5 tons, requiring the replacement of some of the first generation of motorbuses. The LGOC. had inherited from Vanguard an overhaul works at Walthamstow. The next stage in the development of the London motorbus was the manufacture there by the LGOC of its own designs of chassis, developed by its Chief Motor Engineer Frank Searle, and this is related in a subsequent chapter.

Electric Buses

James Whiting

Buses powered by electric batteries have a long history and the first electric bus was built in 1889, eight years before the first one with an internal combustion engine. In both cases these buses were experimental and neither operated in service in London.

The first London bus service to be operated with the use of electric batteries was introduced by the London Electrobus Company, running between Victoria and Liverpool Street, and began on Monday 15th July 1907. The first of these buses had been shown to the press in the latter half of April 1906, when the company ambitiously claimed that 300 of them would be running within the following twelve months. The press information also stated that the electric bus is 'absolutely noiseless, emits no offensive smell or smoke, and is less liable to breakdown'. It was noted also that it was very smooth running. One of the many enthusiastic press reports said 'Other things being equal, the electrically propelled 'bus will inevitably drive the petrol vehicle off the streets'. In the event only six of the buses were built, running at up to 12 miles per hour – at that time the speed limit on London's streets. One was displayed at the 1907 Commercial Vehicle show at Olympia in March.

The Electrobus Company soon found that running these buses did not provide the profit expected. At first the company charged higher fares than its competitors for the smoother ride provided, but after their conductors came in for objections from passengers, it was very quickly necessary for the fares to be reduced to be the same as those of its competitors along the same route. The costs of running the fleet were greater because the company initially had only the six buses and each could operate only six to eight journeys per day, carrying a maximum of 36 passengers (18 on each deck). Arrangements were quickly made, within a month of the service starting, to improve the battery charging facilities so that this number of journeys per bus could be increased. By late 1908 the company had about 20 electric buses in service when it started to run a second route from Victoria to Kilburn. That proved to be its peak.

At the end of November 1908, it was announced that the Electrobuses would soon be equipped with covered top decks. A trial trip with one the buses so equipped was made on the 28th of that month taking a press party at 12.30pm from the Hotel Cecil in the Strand to the City via Ludgate Hill, returning via Queen Victoria Street and the Embankment to the back of the same hotel. *The Globe*, a daily newspaper of the time, reported on 30th November that 'Thanks to the enterprise of the London Electrobus Company, London will soon be provided with motor 'buses with covered-in upper decks similar to those on the electric trams'. It went on to say that this was subject to the approval of the Metropolitan Police, but the reporter saw no reason why they should object in view of the lower centre of gravity of the Electrobus, which would deal with the police's concerns about their perceived risk of double deck buses toppling over with too much weight upstairs. The roof fitted for this trip was intended for summer use, having open sides, and added a weight equivalent to two to three passengers.

The optimism was misplaced. The Metropolitan Police refused to license it for service, perhaps concerned that a planned winter version of the roof, with

The London Electrobus Company started operation from a garage in Horseferry Road, Westminster in 1907, and used up to 20 vehicles until it ceased operation in 1910. LN 701 was one of the batch used on their route to Liverpool Street, and is seen outside the District Railway station at Victoria. Like Premier later, the unnumbered Electrobus route followed LGOC route 11, which continues to this day. A comprehensive display of cigars are on show in the shop to the right. (London Transport Museum)

side windows, would be heavier. There may also perhaps have been some lobbying from the other bus companies running in London, who will undoubtedly have known about this Electrobus development.

The two services lasted through 1909 but came to an end at the start of 1910 when the company went into liquidation. Eight of the vehicles were sold to the Brighton, Hove and Preston United bus company but the rest were broken up for spares. The last Electrobus in Brighton ran in April 1917.

In this view of Electrobus LN 708 the heavy batteries are prominent behind the front wheel. This bus is operating the original route but the advertising on the side, with details of a fares war that Electrobus were involved in, indicates that it dates from after the introduction of the short-lived second route to Brondesbury Station. The buses carried a green and cream livery, as can seen on the back cover.

The battery changing operation at the Electrobus garage in Horseferry Road. A hydraulic ram was used to raise a trolley underneath the bus onto which the spent battery pack was released, and the trolley was then lowered and moved away for the battery to be recharged. A fully charged battery pack was then brought underneath the bus on a trolley and raised into position. The battery packs were stated to weigh around 30 cwt. (around 1,500 kg), and the changing operation only took a few minutes. (Commercial Motor)

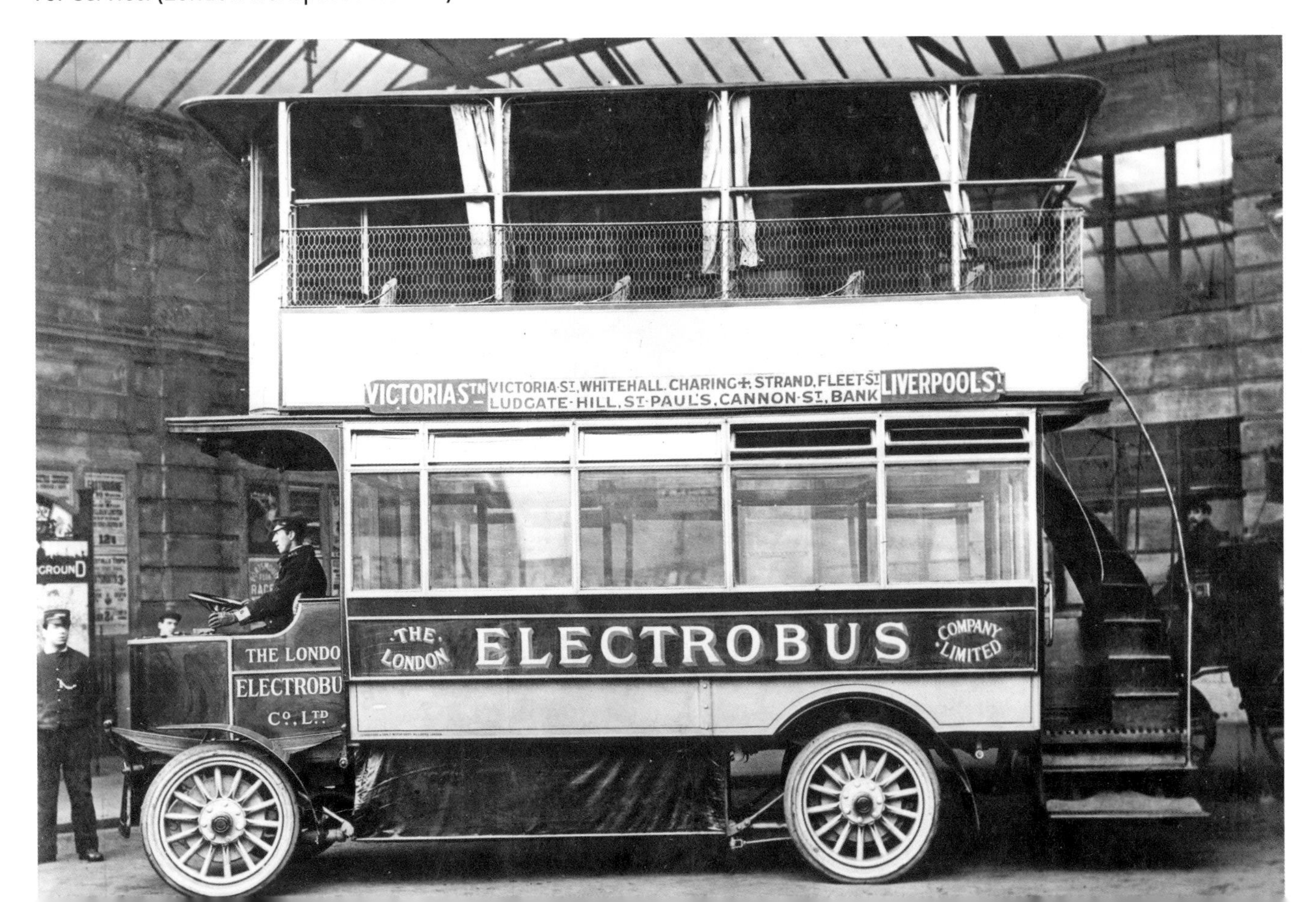

The covered top Electrobus at Victoria Station in 1908. Notwithstanding the lightweight construction of the top deck cover and the massive weight of the batteries underneath the chassis, the Metropolitan Police refused to licence it for service. (London Transport Museum)

The B Type

Mick Webber

Many different types of motor bus had been tried in the capital in the early years of the twentieth century, but at the suggestion of Colonel Frank Searle, the LGOC Chief Motor Engineer, the company decided to design and build its own. It was felt that standardisation was important, and their overhaul works at Walthamstow was the obvious place to build the new vehicle. The result was the X type, which was completed in August 1909. A total of sixty of these were built.

Lessons were learned with this new vehicle, and it was felt that an improved design and specification were needed. The result was the B type, which went into production between 1910 and 1912. During this period B 1 to B 2034 were delivered and the LGOC built the bulk of the bodies, with help from Dodson and Brush, though some of these were fitted with lorry bodies for use in the service vehicle fleet. The legal speed limit at the time was still 12mph, though the B type had an official top speed of 16mph and was capable of more. Initially the interior lighting (electric from 1912) was considered sufficient to light the bus both inside and out, but headlights were added from 1913.

A further six hundred were built in 1913, and another one hundred and fifty in 1914. Included were some single deckers, 90 of which had been built by the end of the First World War, and some of those in service at the start of it were commandeered for use as ambulances. It is well known the important part that the B type bus played in the First World War, when over 900 of the double-deckers were requisitioned for use in Europe. In addition to this, 300 were commandeered for use as lorries on the home front. Many of the buses used overseas never returned.

After the war, 32 B type lorries were fitted with bus bodies and entered service. Two hundred and fifty new buses were built between December 1918 and April 1919 by AEC, some being completed using parts and bodies that had been in store at the start of the war. The LGOC was also allowed to buy back from the War Office 165 of the vehicles that had been commandeered for use at home and a further 230 that had been returned from overseas.

When Chiswick Works was opened in 1921, the buses benefited from a new concept of overhaul which could be applied to a standardised fleet, and relieved garages from much of the work. By 1921, the new K type buses were beginning to impose themselves in London, and there were over a thousand in service by this time. The decline in use of the B type had started. Licensed examples at the end of 1922 were 1,238; in 1923 this total was 1,061, followed by 518 and 447 in 1924 and 1925.

In 1926, only 214 were licensed for service, and when the General Strike was called in May, all of them were withdrawn and sent to Chiswick. They were used on emergency routes and driven by volunteers with police protection. After the strike they returned to their garages, but only briefly as 158 were soon withdrawn and the remainder were retired in August 1927.

The B type will be remembered as the very first standardised London bus built in large quantities, and which allowed easier maintenance using many standard parts. The overhaul system was simplified and more efficient, and the type was the first of many more fleets of standard buses to follow.

The Metropolitan Electric Tramways had entered the bus business when it feared that the new form of transport would threaten their empire. Under an agreement made in 1913, the LGOC agreed to supply the 'MET' with some B type buses from their fleet, and this commenced the same year. Route 105A ran from Ealing to Hook, and B 737 can be seen here at Cleveland Road in Ealing outside Cleveland Park. (Richard Stevenson Collection)

This is The Broadway in West Hendon, and this terrace, opposite Cool Oak Lane, still exists, although in a much less attractive state. The bus is B 957, built in 1911, and working route 58 to Shoreditch, which operated between July 1913 and January 1915. (Richard Stevenson Collection)

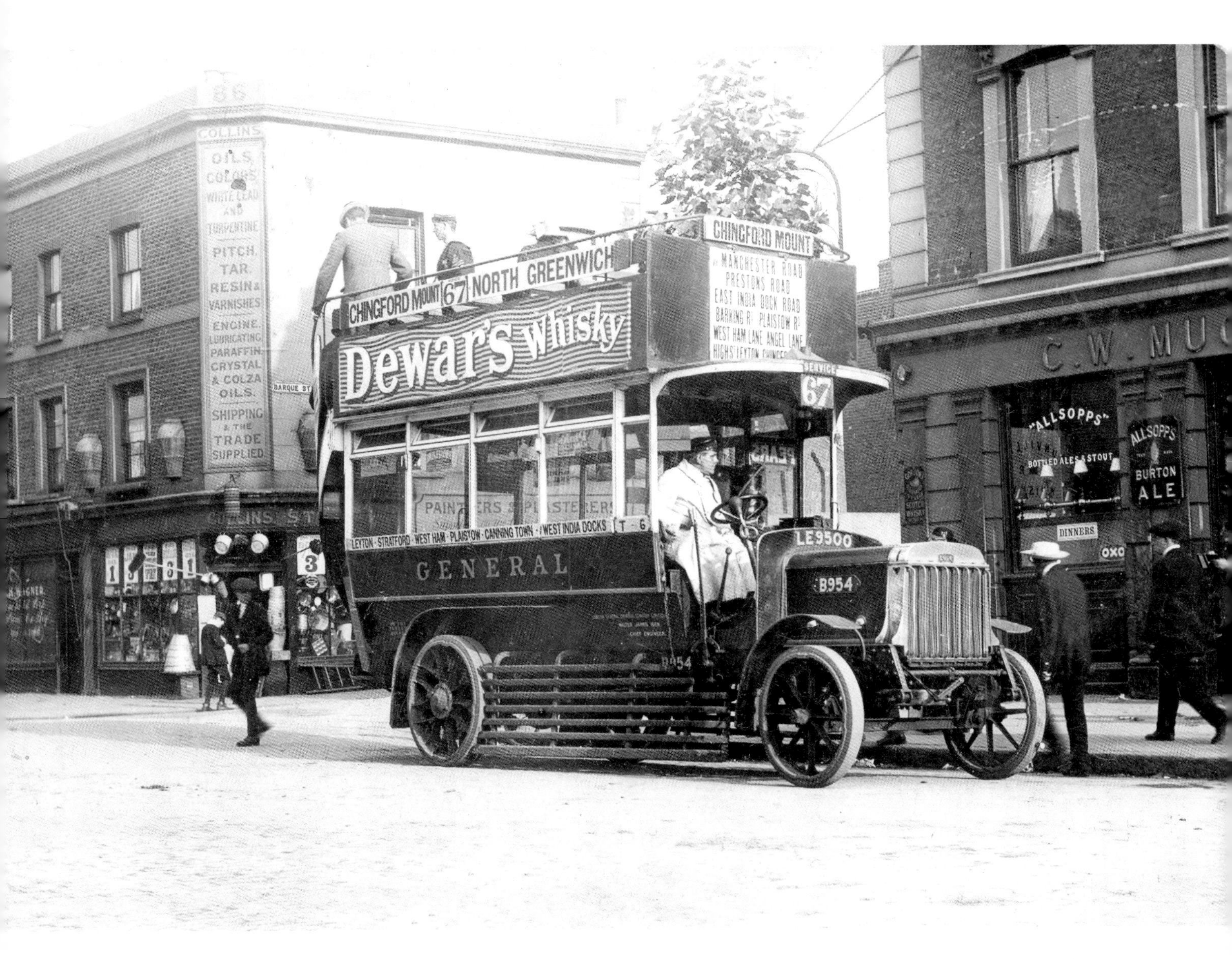

The Isle of Dogs contained the West India and Millwall Docks, and many of the dock workers lived in the terraced houses in this part of east London. This is Manchester Road and B 954, built in 1911, is working from Leyton garage on route 67. The shop on the corner of Barque Street has an informative advert painted on the corner, listing the comprehensive range of goods that can be supplied. This whole area has since been re-developed.

This is Cannon Hill Southgate, by the green. It remains unchanged although not as rural. B 1185 dates from 1911 and heads a queue of five others lined up on the 29 for Victoria. The main central section of this route still runs under that number. The coming of the Piccadilly line to the area in 1933 would change travel in the area forever. (Richard Stevenson Collection)

TO VICTORIA
ALDERMAN'S HILL
PALMER'S GREEN WOOD GREEN
GREEN LANES FINSBURY PARK
SEVEN SISTERS ROAD
CAMDEN TOWN HAMPSTEAD Rᴰ
CHARING +
SOUTHGATE
PINK'S JAMS
MENNEN'S
MENNEN'S
SERVICE
29
GENERAL
MINERALS
LIGHT
REFRESHMENTS
TEAS
ICES
TEAS ICES MINE

A lovely period scene at Piccadilly Circus in about 1912. The statue of Anteros was erected in 1893 to commemorate the work of the 7th Earl of Shaftesbury. Driving here was a free for all at this time, and as can be seen, vehicles and horse traffic were all thrown together at this busy junction. An unidentified Clarkson of the National Steam Car Company is in the centre of the picture, ahead of two LGOC B types, with a further two B types facing each other on the right. (London Transport Museum)

The Metropolitan Steam Omnibus Co. Ltd. was the first significant operator of steam buses in London, starting operation in October 1907. It used Darracq-Serpollet buses, but problems with reliability and obtaining spare parts caused it to switch to conventional petrol-engined motor buses in the second half of 1912. LN 6819 is one of the Darracq-Serpollets, here seen demonstrating a very cumbersome-looking life-saving apparatus of which nothing is known but it was evidently not successful. (Capital Transport Collection)

In 1912, presumably after one or a number of cases of people falling in front of buses, B 2553 was fitted experimentally with this life saving gear. It is probable that it never entered service. (Capital Transport Collection)

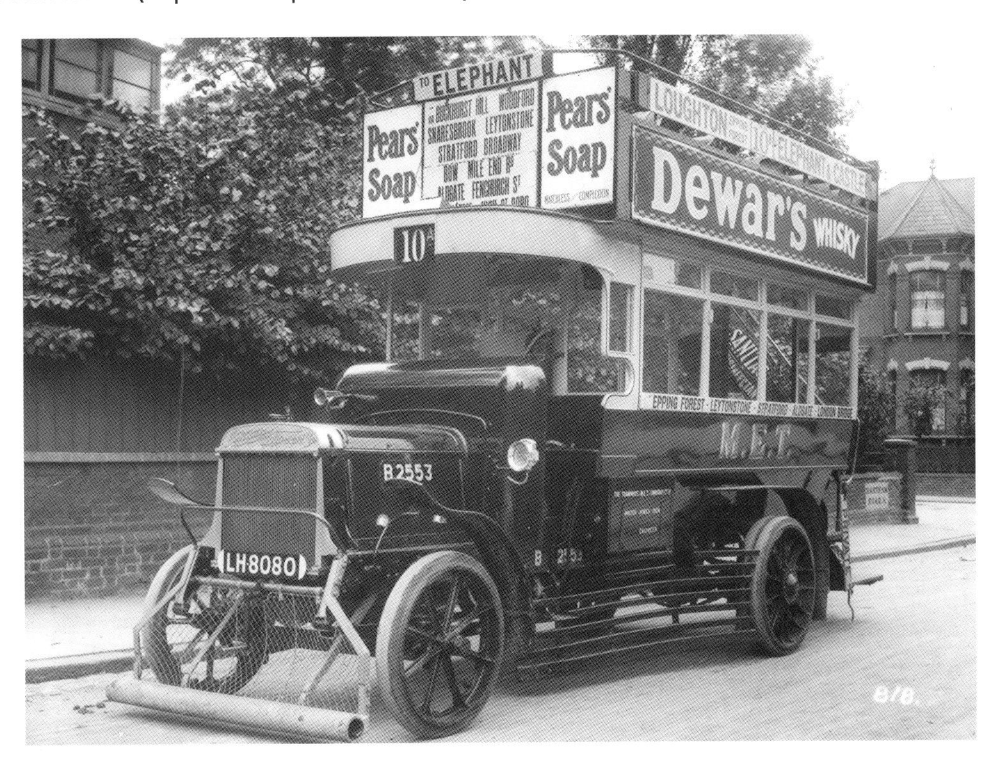

This is Marble Arch in about 1912.. There is obviously no rule of the road here, it is a question of point the vehicle and go! B 937 was built in 1911, and the driver heads towards the Edgware Road on route 16. Coming towards him from the distance is General X 4 on the 32 bound for Ladbroke Grove. The X type was the predecessor to the B type, and sixty were built from 1909. On the far right are LGOC route 16 bus tickets from 1912, during which year the design changed. (Ferodo Ltd and Laurie Akehurst Collection)

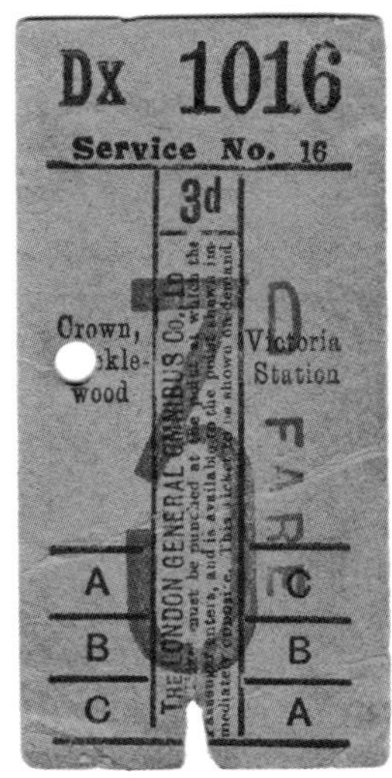

Eq 5006

SERVICE 16

1d

Willesden Garage	Crown, Cricklewood
Crown, Cricklewood	
Mill Lane	Elgin Avenue
	St. Johns Wood Road
	Chapel Street
Elgin Avenue	Oxford Street
Chapel Street	St. Georges Hospital
Oxford Street	Victoria Station
Victoria Station	Chelsea Town Hall
Sloane Square	Wellington Rd Battersea
A	D
B	E
C	F

THE LONDON GENERAL OMNIBUS CO. LTD.

Route 73 was a long cross London route between Stoke Newington and Richmond. In this view, B 1865 appears to be driverless and the man standing to the right of the bus seems puzzled! An LCC E class car built in 1906 trundles off in the opposite direction to its terminus on route 43. The pub on the right is on the corner of Cazenove Road at Stamford Hill, and has since been restored and converted to a shop. (Richard Stevenson Collection)

This is Reigate, and soldiers march through the town. Could they be on their way to war, or perhaps coming home? People have turned out to see them, and ladies are in their finery. The bus, B 1489 from 1912, waits on route 160 to make its way to Stockwell with a full load, and perhaps Charlwood's tea rooms over the road will do some business soon. (Richard Stevenson Collection)

During the First World War, a large proportion of the London General fleet were commandeered by the War Department as troop transport. One of the many assembly points was at Grove Park in south east London.
Two line-ups of B types can be seen here, newly painted in khaki, and minus registration plates, ready to depart for the Western front. Although many were destroyed or scrapped, quite a few returned to service after the hostilities.

Bank holidays were a good excuse to jump on a bus and get away for a few hours. This scene at Chislehurst in 1921, shows a long queue waiting for a ride. B 2651 had been used by the War department during the war, and had been renovated and placed back into service in 1919. It looks as though it is already full and ready to depart for Charing Cross, and so the crowd will have to be patient and wait for the next bus. (Richard Stevenson Collection)

It is Whit Monday 1921, and this is the scene at Venn Street, Clapham Common, where the 125-minute journey to Dorking on route 107 is proving extremely popular.. B 1325 already has a full load, and it will need many more buses to shift the crowds. It is apparent that you weren't dressed properly if you didn't have a hat! Dorking, and nearby Boxhill, was a very popular destination on Bank Holiday weekends. (Mick Webber Collection)

DORKING
BALHAM HIGH ROAD
TOOTING BROADWAY
NORTH CHEAM EWELL
EPSOM ASHTEAD
LF 8105
SWEETS
& ICES
MOTOR VANS
FOR HIRE
GOODS REMOVED

Bus garages from all over London sent privately hired buses to the Epsom downs for Derby Day. In addition, special services were operated on existing local routes. The three buses identifiable are B 977, from Battersea, with B 2310 and B 811. It would be very difficult to spot anyone in view that is not wearing a hat! Several open top charabancs are in the foreground, but it is the double deck vehicles that afford the best views. (London Transport Museum)

MANN CROSSMAN'S
OATMEAL STOUT
USE
LUX
WON'T SHRINK WOOLLENS
DUNLOP TYRES
SOLID & PNEUMATIC FOR ALL MOTOR VEHICLES
PRIVATE HIRE DEPARTMENT
DAILY SKETCH
WHIST DRIVE
Pears' WHITE OPAQUE
is One
FIRST

The Next Developments

Andrew Robertson

At the end of the First World War the LGOC had an urgent need for new buses to replace those which had not returned after war service and to expand services. Two hundred and fifty new B-types were built in 1919, but the 34 seats of the B-type represented the maximum capacity which could be achieved within the constraints of Metropolitan Police limits on the length and weight of buses. To achieve greater capacity required engineering innovation, and the first of a new generation of buses, K 1, appeared in August 1919. By changing from normal control, with the driver positioned behind the engine, to forward control, with the driver seated alongside and above the engine, the front bulkhead could be brought forward. The body was wider and straight-sided, allowing transverse instead of longitudinal seats on the lower deck, while the upper deck protruded slightly over the driver's position. This decisive break from the traditional horse bus style body allowed seating to be increased to a total of 46.

The London General introduced the new "K" type bus in 1919. It differed greatly from the familiar "B" type in that the driver was seated next to the engine, rather than behind it, and it seated 46 rather than 34 on its predecessor. K 1 is pictured on 3rd September 1919 boarded up for route 11 at Liverpool Street.. The first batch of the production run were to follow in eight months' time. (Capital Transport Collection)

Finsbury Park in the 1920s. Beyond the 'normal control' B types are two K types with the greater passenger accommodation. The single-decker is almost as tall as the double-decker. The bodies were interchangeable with the double-deck ones and some swapping of bodies to chassis occurred. The single-deck Bs were of various body designs which had seating for between 16 and 26 passengers.

Over 1,100 K-types were built, but in 1920 the Police increased the maximum permitted weight to 8 tons, which allowed a larger design to be produced. This was the S-type, which seated 54, and the first of these entered service in December 1920. Over 900 S-types were built between 1920 and 1927.

Although double-deckers were always the norm in London, low bridges, weight limits and other infrastructure requirements made single-deck operation necessary on a few routes. The first single-deck motor bus route in London (apart from the very first motor buses) was route 69, between Plumstead and Poplar via the Blackwall Tunnel, introduced in November 1912. The 69 used a small fleet of B-types with specially constructed single-deck bodies. More B-type single-deckers followed, and small numbers of both K-types and S-types were also built with single-deck bodies.

OFF LICENSE
SPIRITS
FANCY DRAPERY
STH CROYDON
BOROUGH ELEPHANT
STREATHAM COMMON
HEINZ SALAD CREAM
DUNLOP

The London General K class buses came into service mainly from May 1920, and were delivered in three large batches. The first batch was from K 4 to K 503. The bus here on the right is K 403. One thousand and forty chassis were produced in the first year alone! The two buses in this view are operating on route 86 from Liverpool Street to South Croydon, and follow the tram lines along Whitehorse Road in Croydon. (Richard Stevenson Collection)

LGOC B-type and K-type buses on the newly-constructed North Circular Road carrying spectators to Wembley Stadium on 28th April 1923 for the first-ever FA Cup Final to be held there. On the left is empty K type bus K 809 (XC 8406) on route 53, followed by B 1816 (LF 8577) and B 1233 (LF 8013) operating private hires, the latter with a top deck full of passengers. More buses are visible in the background, including another B-type operating route 16 and other traffic includes a taxi, charabanc and horse and cart. The 16 and 53 were among six routes specially extended to Wembley for the day. The match itself was won by Bolton Wanderers, who beat West Ham United 2-0. (London Transport Museum)

Route 12B was a variant of route 12 introduced in 1922. By 1924 it was operating between East Acton and Lower Sydenham, but under the complex route numbering scheme introduced by Chief Constable Bassom under the London Traffic Act 1924 it was renumbered 112. A K Type is seen on the newly introduced gyratory traffic scheme at Parliament Square on 16th June 1926. What is today the UK's Supreme Court is seen on the right. (London Transport Museum)

TO EPSOM RACE COURSE
STONECOT HILL
NORTH CHEAM
EWELL
REIGATE ROAD
LONGDOWN LANE
164A
BRITISH MADE
SWAN
VESTAS
SPECIALLY MADE FOR SMOKERS
BRITISH MADE
SWAN
VESTAS
SPECIALLY MADE FOR SMOKERS
GENERAL
LU 8511

Derby Day at Epsom was a time when extras were operated on many local routes. Route 164 worked a circular from Morden via Ewell, Sutton and Rose Hill, but the 164A was a race day route from Morden to the racecourse. The two buses on this route are K 356 and K 957, and they are about to pass Midland Red 1926 SOS type charabanc HA 3521. The weather doesn't look too favourable, and top coats are the order of the day. (London Transport Museum)

This is the Strand at the Aldwych, with Waterloo Bridge to the left. It is the mid-twenties, and K and S type buses dominate with S350 on route 96 to the left, and K 832 in the foreground on route 6. The once common B type was in decline, and a solitary one can be seen in front of the S type. All B types had been withdrawn by the end of 1927. The Strand links the cities of Westminster and London, and comes from the old English word "strond" which means edge of the river. (London Transport Museum)

K 191 was the first of 12 K-types to be fitted with this experimental top-deck windscreen in August 1922, but they did not last long in service. It will be noted that in accordance with Metropolitan Police requirements the driver still has no protection against the elements other than a tarpaulin.

Route 171 linked Kingston with Chertsey via Thames Ditton, Weybridge and Addlestone.
This July 1929 view shows K 32 in Kingston on a wet day, and the driver open to the elements. The single deck version of the K type first appeared in 1925, although the bus pictured was originally a double decker that had a newer single deck body mounted on its chassis.
(W.Noel Jackson/Alan Cross)

The New Independents – 1922

Ken Blacker (first published in *Old Motor* magazine in 1972)

It is 1922 and the London General Omnibus Company had been bitterly criticised in recent times for the serious inadequacy of many of its services. But the shortage of buses following the First World War was now easing considerably and the company was gradually improving matters. Except for the municipal tramways, the Underground combine (of which the LGOC was a part) had things all its own way on the streets of London and was anxious to retain this position, but things were about to change. Its officials were told to discreetly find out more about a new bus to be placed in service by a competitor - a brown and cream Leyland called *Express*. Harry Webb of Tillings – who worked hand in glove with the LGOC – tracked it down to Leyland's London depot and confirmed the fact that it belonged to a taxi driver called A G Partridge and that it was about to appear for plating by the police at the end of July 1922. After minor alterations the police passed it fit for London and unofficially expressed the view that no better bus had ever been placed before them.

The original *Chocolate Express* took to the road on August 5th 1922. The national newspapers gave it the fullest publicity; understandably, perhaps, since it worked usually on the famous route 11 which passed along the length of Fleet Street. The General gave it close scrutiny too. Specially picked crews were detailed to work in convoy immediately ahead of and behind it wherever it went and officials, in uniform and plain clothes, watched its every move. The "chasers" fore and aft of the *Chocolate Express* made life very difficult for Partridge and his partners but, luckily for them, General soon had to bow to public opinion and withdraw them.

The *Chocolate Express* triggered off the reaction that the LGOC feared most. Its exploits were glamourised and the inevitable result was that others decided to follow suit. There was a trickle of newcomers at first. S H Hole of Samuelsons was followed by men like the clever but heavy drinking Percy Frost Smith, the ebullient George Adams of the *Primrose* and the ill-fated Bernard Cosgrove of *Admiral* whose confused personal life later wrecked his career and ended in suicide. The trickle became a stream, and by the end of 1923 the stream had become a torrent. Even the top echelon at Electric Railway House could not have foreseen that by the end of 1925 there would be over six hundred independent buses on London streets.

General and their associates were powerless to stop the invasion. There was no licensing system for bus services and, provided the police approved a vehicle for a route, it could run on it as and when its owner liked. Many of the new busmen obtained approval for whole selections of routes over which they roamed at will, going wherever there were likely to be the most passengers and all too often depositing existing passengers at the kerbside in order to turn round and take a bigger load back the other way. The newspapers and Lord Ashfield dubbed them "pirates" and this

The Chocolate Express Omnibus Company was one of the better known London Independent bus operators. It was founded by three ex-servicemen, and their first bus was delivered in 1922. The vehicle pictured here is UC 8658, which is a Leyland with bodywork built by Dodson in 1928. It is seen here in the Strand on the 11B bound for Victoria. The company was taken over by the LPTB and left the London streets in August 1934. (Capital Transport)

"VICTORIA Stn"
STRAND CHARING +
VICTORIA SLOANE Sq
KINGS Rd WALHAM Gn
HAMMERSMITH Bdy
GINGER
ALE
11
UC 8658
KEITH
PROWSE
SWAN VEST
THE BEST VALUE
TRY THE
NEW
POWER
PETROL
7.047

name stuck. Many of the more responsible independent proprietors resented this and regarded it as an unwarranted stigma; they were serving Londoners' needs just as much as was the combine. But, in truth, there were just as many whose methods of working were grossly unsatisfactory and because of them the independents began to get a bad name.

Who were they, these independent bus owners? A few were existing garage proprietors. Many more were taxicab owners whose trade was suffering a recession and who turned to buses as a similar line of business. One or two successful businessmen with fingers in several pies, like William Moriarty of the *Claremont* and Charles H Pickup, owned buses as part of their wider interests. Existing coach companies such as South London Coaches and Julius & Lockwood sometimes bought a bus or two. Others were started by ex-LGOC staff and *Horseshoe* was run by a one-time tram conductor. Several private bus owners were young ex-servicemen with no transport background and no prospects of secure and

The Primrose fleet consisted of four buses, and No 1 was this Straker-Squire new in 1922 with Straker bodywork. Although not showing a route number, it appears to be following the General route 11, and is being followed by LGOC S 357 on that route. It was discarded in 1927. Note that the bus manufacturer has made use of the vehicle to advertise their products. (Mick Webber Collection)

interesting employment elsewhere. Lured by reputed big profits many used their army gratuity to finance the first instalment on the purchase of a bus.

There were five main types of bus available to the independents in 1922-6 and all had to pass the highly stringent tests of the Metropolitan Police before they were allowed to enter service. And each had to be overhauled and re-examined annually. Only two operators, Samuelson and Cambrian Landray, converted existing charabancs into double-deckers, the latter's Tilling Stevens sharing with Percy Frost Smith's six home-made chassis the honour of being the only independent petrol electrics. All the others bought from Leyland, Straker Squire, Thornycroft or Dennis, or else they bought reconditioned ex-War Department Daimlers from Josiah M Roberts' Cathnor Motor Works at Shepherd's Bush. Perhaps the best allrounder was the Dennis, but it did not come into the picture until August 1923 after which it sold in large quantities. The Leyland was equally fast and reliable but was dearer and often late on delivery.

The Stevens Brothers started the Pioneer Omnibus Company with the purchase of a Thornycroft 50 seater in July 1923. At the time, it was the largest seating capacity bus being operated by any independent in the capital. This bus is seen here on route 73 in Oxford Street between Marble Arch and Portman Street, with a London General K type following on the 2A. The Ideal Studios on the right was a popular place for people to call in for their portrait to be taken for the family album. The LPTB took over the Pioneer operations in December 1933.

Earlier ones had a turning circle which was unsatisfactory for many London routes. The semi forward-control Straker Squire was possibly the fastest of all but notorious for its unreliability. Thornycroft produced the only really forward-control vehicle with the high seating capacity of fifty, but it was as slow and ponderous as the K and S types of General and did not find wide acclaim. Roberts's Daimlers defy categorisation. Some were good; many were abominably bad with life spans as low as one year. F F Downes of the *Horseshoe* and possibly others were helped to financial ruin by the Daimlers and some, including *Cosmopolitan* and *Peraeque*, their patience exhausted, returned them to Shepherd's Bush and fought out legal battles over them afterwards.

The antics of the independents began to worry the police, who also had the problem of mounting traffic congestion to contend with. The General and its associates were able to lobby in high places for the situation to be controlled, and declining receipts on tramway routes flooded by independent buses led the councils to demand action. The result was the London Traffic Act of 1924 which decreed that all buses operating within the Metropolitan Police area must operate strictly to schedules deposited with and approved by the police.

These schedules could not be varied without police permission. From the independents' point of view the worst feature of the Act was Section 7 which allowed the police to nominate streets as "restricted", and once so nominated the number of scheduled buses on them could not be increased. Indeed, the police had powers to compel existing buses to be withdrawn if they wished. The Restricted Streets Orders of 1925 onwards, which were often retrospective, soon began to bite. They effectively put a stop to the entry into service of additional buses as most of the routes likely to be profitable soon had restricted streets on them. The momentum of new buses and operators slowed appreciably from early 1925 onwards and such extra buses as were placed into service were generally to be found on still-unrestricted suburban roads. There were never any restrictions on Sundays and bank holidays when bus operators were allowed to continue the free-for-all subject to depositing the necessary schedules. The 1924 Act meant that each weekday schedule became a valuable commodity and started the second phase in the independent story. General began to buy out the independents whenever the opportunity arose in order to obtain their schedules.

General's business and financial position had deteriorated badly in 1923 and 1924 and this was almost entirely due to the competition which, with few exceptions, creamed the most profitable routes. There were comparatively few instances where they covered completely new territory. The combine had been forced by public opinion to abandon the strategy of allocating two "chasers" to each independent at a very early stage and was left with only one alternative, to flood the busiest routes with buses of its own to bring down the receipts on each bus to an uneconomic level and thus force the private men out of business. Before long Londoners had a level of bus service they had never known before. One route alone, the 29 from Victoria to the Cherry Tree at Southgate, could boast at peak times a combined frequency of over two buses a minute, not to mention the tram service which ran parallel for much of its length. Inevitably the weaker independents began to fall by the wayside and for them the passing of the London Traffic Act was the last straw. Many were glad to sell out to General who were not ungenerous in paying about £2000 for each scheduled bus.

Things changed dramatically when a newcomer appeared on the scene in July 1927 in the form of the London Public

The fleetname X Service was intended to signify that the proprietors were ex-servicemen, and they used a khaki and red livery to emphasise the point. Started by L. St. E. S. Punnett, C.G. Kemp-Small and C.S. Clarke in 1923, the latter two soon dropped out leaving Punnett as the sole owner of the company. X Service only ever owned two Straker-Squires, of which the second, XR 8763, is seen here. X Service operated from Dangerfield's garages in Camden High Street and Harmood Street, Chalk Farm, but ceased operation in July 1925. (Capital Transport Collection)

E. Puttergill Ltd ran buses under the names of Shanghai and Golden Arrow. One of the former is seen here, XU 5585, which was a Dennis 48 seater built in August 1924. This Kings Cross view shows the vehicle waiting time for its return to Richmond on the 73A, with the 1850s train shed as a backdrop. The company was swallowed up by the LPTB in November 1933. (W. Noel Jackson/ Alan Cross)

THE BALD
FACED
STAG
THE
BALD.FACED.STAG
PALE
CANNON
ALES
Wine & Spirit Merchant
SALOON BAR
STOP

A nice sunny day in High Road East Finchley, and The Bald Faced Stag pub on the left, proudly displays its mascot looking down on proceedings. The buildings in view are all still intact. East End Road is on the left beyond the Bald Faced Stag, and Fortis Green leads off towards Muswell Hill on the right. The bus is owned by Overground, and was their number 18, a Dennis with Dodson 48-seat body, built in January 1925 and working their route 284 to Victoria. (Richard Stevenson Collection)

Omnibus Company Ltd operated by A T Bennett whose fleet of Admiral buses was put under its control. Public let it be known that it intended to develop into a strong independent undertaking by absorbing existing operators who were free to buy shares in it. Many who viewed the future with a degree of gloom but were loathe to sell out to the combine took advantage of Public's offer to buy their business. It was paying between £500 and £1000 more per scheduled bus than the LGOC and this made the offer very tempting indeed. Only those with a burning desire to remain independent could afford to turn down an offer of £3000 a bus, which was irrespective of its age and condition. In 1928, after Public had acquired two hundred scheduled buses, it became known that the financing of the company was guaranteed by General, and in 1929 it was absorbed by them. Over 130 fleet names disappeared from London streets between 1925 and 1928, though a few lingered temporarily as reminders of the past on standard LGOC vehicles which had replaced the non-standard types inherited with the acquired independent fleets.

The independents were an imaginative lot when it came to choosing fleet names. The derivation of some was obvious, like *Havaride*, *Uneedus*, *Rapid* and *Essential*. Others were less obvious. *Cornwall* would seem an unusual name for a London bus unless you happened to know that the owner's address was Cornwall Road. *Fairlop*, *Henslow* and others derived their names similarly. The British Empire Exhibition of 1924/5 brought out a patriotic fervour which probably accounted for the various Empires, Imperials and, of course, *Empire's Best*. Pure frivolity resulted in *Royal Toots* and *Tally Ho!* whilst a secondary school education probably helped in dreaming up names like *Peraeque* and *Pro Bono Publico*. Surprisingly few owners used their own names. though Pickup naturally used his as it was particularly appropriate and a few others like Ryan and Martin were exceptions to the general rule.

It has often been written that the independents added a new dimension to the London scene. To a degree this was true but only for a short period. Initially there were some most attractive colour schemes to contrast with the red of General and most of its associates. *Glen* was peach and white, *Invicta* pale blue and *Timpson* silver, to list but a few. But they quickly found that a section of the travelling public, whose natural distrust of anything new was enhanced by rumours – some justified – of irresponsible behaviour by the independents, steered clear of highly coloured buses. So many took the natural step of repainting their vehicles similar to General's on the first or second overhaul. Thus Adam's *Primrose* buses concluded their career painted red, and so did many others. After 1929 the only independent colour to break the monotony of reds and chocolates was the handsome light brown of the *City*, Birch and United buses, most of which were on route 536.

Just a few years later, the London Passenger Transport Act of 1933 meant that monopoly was to be restored to passenger transport in the capital. Private enterprise was to cease; the bonanza was over. Lord Ashfield had never eased up his verbal onslaught on the independents even though, by 1929, their activities were fully stabilised and carried out with as much regard to the public's needs as were those of the combine. Indeed some gave a personal service second to none as their regular riders would be quick to testify.

Sixty-four London independent operators remained to the end, running 169 schedules. The first compulsory acquisitions by the LPTB occurred on 1st November 1933 and the last 'pirate' of all, a Leyland Titan of the Prince Omnibus Company, ran into its garage in the early hours of 5th December 1934.

Some Birch Brothers buses used the fleetname "Archway", and XX 5044 was one. This Leyland with in house built body, was new in 1925, and can be seen here in Holland Park Avenue on route 526 in 1928. It left the fleet in 1930. (J.B.Atkinson)

This Leyland LB4 with Strachan and Brown bodywork dates from 1924, and the fleet name "Carswool" was derived from the owner's names Woolvett and Carswell. It was the only bus they ever owned, and was transferred to the LPTB in 1933. It is pictured at Turnpike Lane. (J.F.Higham)

Second to None

Mick Webber

In a short time after the appearance of the S-type, yet another new class was introduced, the NS. This was a larger vehicle, and production began in May 1923.

NS 1 was built with a removable roof and, when submitted for inspection, the Metropolitan Police would not pass the vehicle for service unless the roof was removed. This meant that the bus would continue to be at a disadvantage compared with the trams, which were now mostly running with top deck covers. The Police deemed that buses with roofs made the vehicles top heavy. Despite this, the NS went ahead, initially with open tops, orders soon being placed for both chassis and bodies, the bodies being shared between a number of companies including Short Brothers, Brush, Ransome Sims and Jefferies and the LGOC. By mid-1925 NS numbers exceeded 1,700.

The company would not give up on having roofs fitted to the class, and in October 1925, the Police agreed to a trial with buses so fitted from Loughton garage on route 100. Approval for them was given and the LGOC ordered 200 more in January 1926, which began to enter service from March.

The next improvement with the class happened in 1928, when pneumatic tyres were fitted. The big plus here was that the speed limit was increased from 12 mph to 20 mph, slashing journey times on many routes. The final improvement to the NS came in 1929, when the driver's cab was given a glazed front. This was not an immediate success, though why is not known, but by May 1931 a new style of cab enclosure was approved and at last the driver was protected from the elements. Previously a Metropolitan Police regulation forbade the licensing of any vehicle completely enclosing the driver in which he would be prevented from seeing or hearing adequately what was passing around him outside. The last NS to enter service in February 1930 was NS 2290, although the highest fleet number was NS 2411. The covered top NS gave the LGOC a significant competitive advantage over the independents, since the chassis most favoured by the independents, the Dennis 45hp and the Leyland LB, were not suitable for fitting covered top bodies. The first independent covered top bus was a six-wheeled Guy which entered service with Public in September 1927, while Thomas Tilling did not start to experiment with covered tops until 1929.

Against the trend, independent operator Charles H Pickup purchased five AEC Regents with open-top bodies as late as 1932, his view being that they encouraged tourist traffic on his operations on Sundays. They were taken over by the LPTB in November 1933, becoming STL 553-557. They continued to operate as open-toppers until they were converted to covered top at Chiswick in 1934.

The NS class survived to be included in the new LPTB fleet when they took over in July 1933, and the very last to run in service was NS 1974 on 30th November 1937. The class was followed by other standard types, starting with the ST and LT, and later the STL. Some of the NS class finished their lives converted to staff canteens, the last of which was retired in 1951.

The NS class marked the transition from the first generation of motor buses towards the modern bus. There was a suggestion that NS stood for "no step", but the LGOC had always insisted that it stood for "nulli secundus" – the Latin for "second to none".

The NS chassis had been designed to allow for covered top decks to be fitted, but the Metropolitan Police continued to refuse authority to operate covered-top buses. The LGOC built NS 1734 to 1737 in 1925 in an attempt to persuade the Police to change their requirements. Initially refused permission to operate on routes 21 and then 88 through central London, the Police relented to permit experimental operation on route 100B between Elephant & Castle and Loughton, and they entered service on 1st October 1925. Here NS 1737 is seen in the Essex countryside. (London Transport Museum)

Compared to the wooden seats of open-top buses, with only a tarpaulin as protection from rain, the top-deck interiors of the new covered-top NSs with upholstered seats, as seen here, must have seemed the height of luxury. (London Transport Museum)

NS 558, new in August 1923 and seen here at Herne Hill while working from Chalk Farm garage, shows the original NS open-top design with open cab. (Omnibus Society)

At Golders Green station, Hendon garage's NS 1108 shows the benefits of its open top for a trip to St Albans through the countryside on a dry day – though taller passengers would have needed to beware of any overhanging trees on the journey. (London Transport Museum)

NS 1226 stands at Crystal Palace Parade while operating a short journey on route 108, demonstrating the enclosed cab which was fitted to NSs from May 1931 onwards. The standard NS body which it carries would have been prohibited from passing through the Blackwall Tunnel, but this journey is only heading as far as the Ship & Billet in Greenwich, an unusual short working which appears to have escaped being given a number under the Bassom numbering system; it may have been an occasion when the Blackwall Tunnel was closed. (Omnibus Society)

NS 130 shows the penultimate stage of the evolution of the NS, with covered top and enclosed cab, but still on solid tyres. It is operating route 37D, a Saturday afternoon extension of the 37 group from Peckham to Old Kent Road, The Wellington, introduced on 19th May 1934 in the last months of the Bassom route numbering system. The General fleetname still survived at this time, since it was only during 1934 that London Transport began to use its own name in place of General as its fleetname. (Omnibus Society)

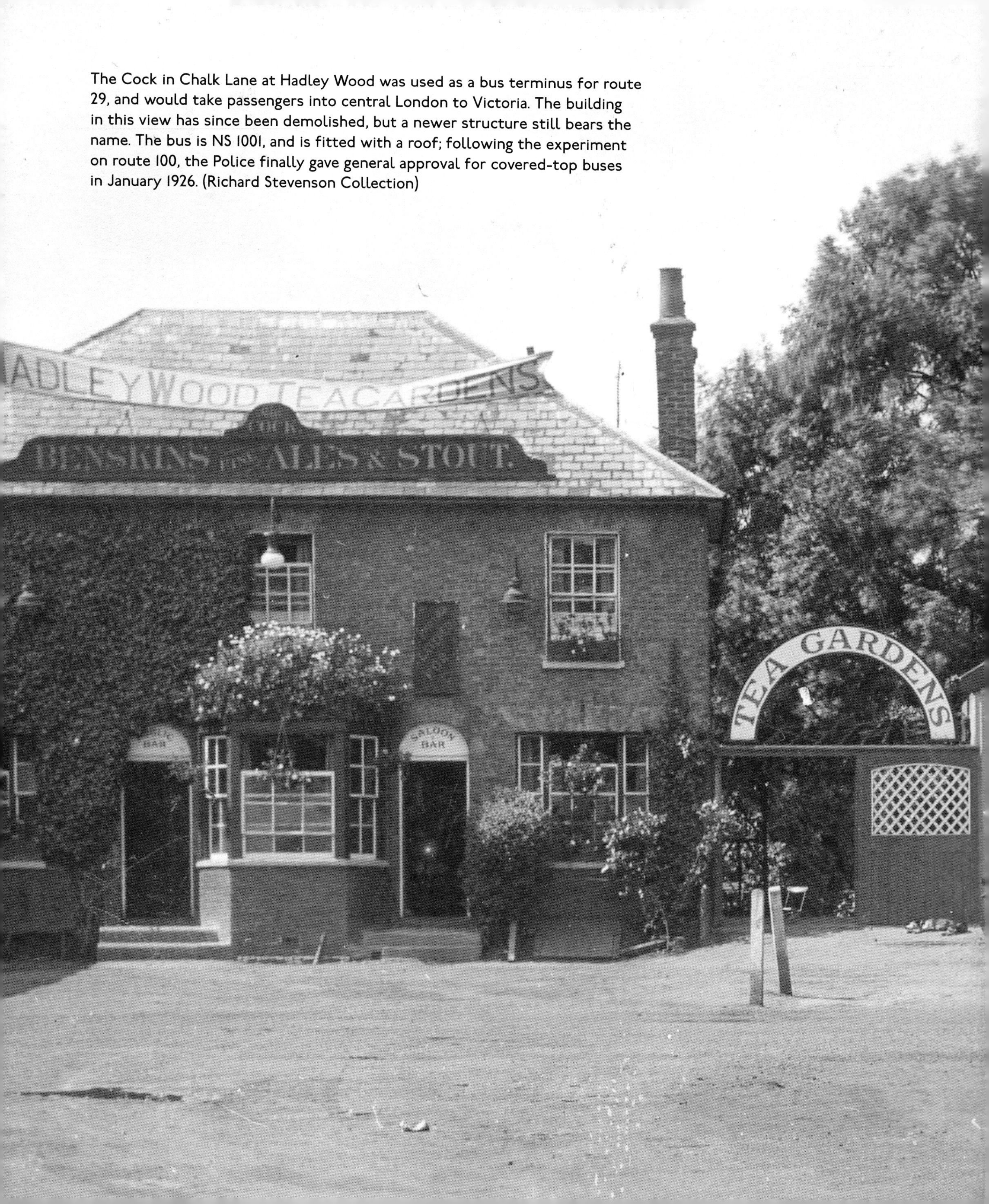

The Cock in Chalk Lane at Hadley Wood was used as a bus terminus for route 29, and would take passengers into central London to Victoria. The building in this view has since been demolished, but a newer structure still bears the name. The bus is NS 1001, and is fitted with a roof; following the experiment on route 100, the Police finally gave general approval for covered-top buses in January 1926. (Richard Stevenson Collection)

VICTORIA STATION
ALDERMANS HILL
GREEN LANES FINSBURY PK
CAMDEN TN HAMPSTEAD RD
PALMERS GREEN WOOD GREEN
SEVEN SISTERS ROAD
CHARING ✠ WHITEHALL
29
GENERAL
GENERAL
XP 6693

This is Hyde Park Corner on 3rd June 1929. The London General had proposed to introduce a six wheeled bus to the London streets, and in May 1927 it was announced that the new bus had arrived, and would seat 68 passengers. This was the LS class, and although only 12 were built, which included one single decker, it paved the way for the new LT class two years later. Looking a bit like the rear of an NS, LS 5, working from Mortlake garage, fights its way through the traffic on route 33A on its way to Richmond. The bus was withdrawn in 1937. (London Transport Museum)

Back cover: Three of the many liveries to be seen on London buses in the early motor bus period, with Electrobus being appropriately green long before the environmental movement.